NON BINARY:

WHAT DO YOU MEAN?

LEE-ANNE LAWRANCE

Published by Rising Moon Books
Dorset, UK
www.therisingmoon.co.uk

Printed in the UK using paper from sustainable sources

ISBN: 978-1-910616-88-8

"Today, I'm marching for that part of me that was once

TOO AFRAID TO MARCH

and for all the people who can't march,

the people living lives like I did.

Today, I march to remember that

I'M NOT JUST A ME. I'M ALSO A WE.

And we march with **PRIDE**."

Nomi Marks
SENS8

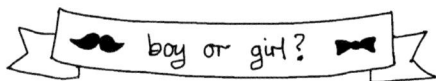

boy or girl?

Hello, friend! ^‿^

INTRODUCTION

IF YOU'VE PICKED UP THIS BOOK YOU'RE PROBABLY LOOKING FOR SOME ANSWERS.

Perhaps you're asking yourself some difficult questions, or perhaps you've been given this book by a friend or family member to help you understand their experience.

IN THIS BOOK YOU'LL FIND EVERYTHING YOU NEED TO HELP YOU ANSWER THE QUESTION:

NON-BINARY?
WHAT DO YOU MEAN?

Ideas about gender have changed a lot, from **CORSETS AND A STIFF UPPER LIP**, to **TRANSGENDER SUPERSTARS** in just over a hundred years! Even in our own lifetime things sometimes seem to be changing so fast we often barely have time to question ideas before another one comes along . . .

But while we are happy to acknowledge that **SEXUALITY** is something that's a moveable feast, we're only at the beginning of realising that not everyone experiences **GENDER** in the same way.

When people experience a gender identity which falls outside traditional definitions, they often have a hard time explaining to others the depth and intensity of their feelings.

THIS BOOK AIMS TO HELP DISPEL SOME OF THE MYTHS AND EXPLAIN SOME OF THE KEY POINTS, whether you're exploring your own gender or trying to understand someone else's.

We have tried not to be too prescriptive - you will be asked to consider

SHADES OF MEANING AND SPECTRUMS OF POSSIBILITY!

The fact is that we're only just beginning to find the words and language around gender to be able to discuss it, and each person may chose slightly different words or comparisons to describe their experiences.

We've tried here to use some of the common words and definitions, and there is a glossary towards the back of the book to help you with some of these terms. There's also your **VERY OWN QUIZ SHEET** to help you or your non-binary friend choose their own terms and pronouns.

ENJOY READING, AND GOOD LUCK ON YOUR GENDER JOURNEY!

Chella Adgopul, Editor

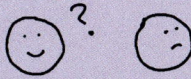

WHAT IS NON-BINARY?

Non-binary is an umbrella term meaning

ANYONE WHO DOES NOT WHOLLY IDENTIFY AS A MAN OR A WOMAN 100% OF THE TIME.

This may sound confusing but it helps if you think of gender as a **SPECTRUM** or a **CONTINUUM**.

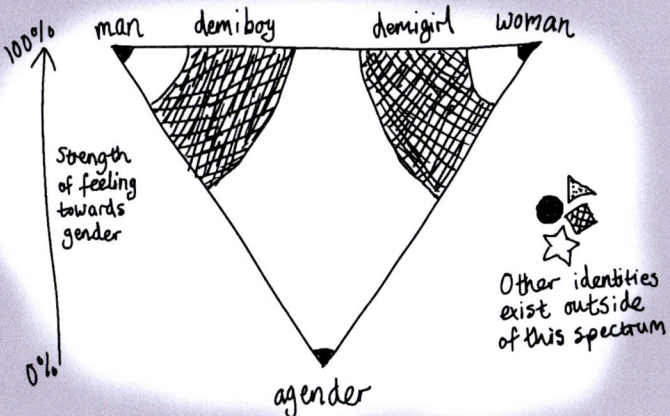

100%

man   demiboy   demigirl   woman

Strength
of feeling
towards
gender

0%

Other identities
exist outside
of this spectrum

agender

Other ways of mapping gender involve sliders. This way, **YOU CAN MOVE EACH SLIDER INDEPENDENTLY.**

Mark each slider to indicate strength of feeling or association:

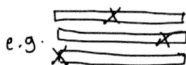

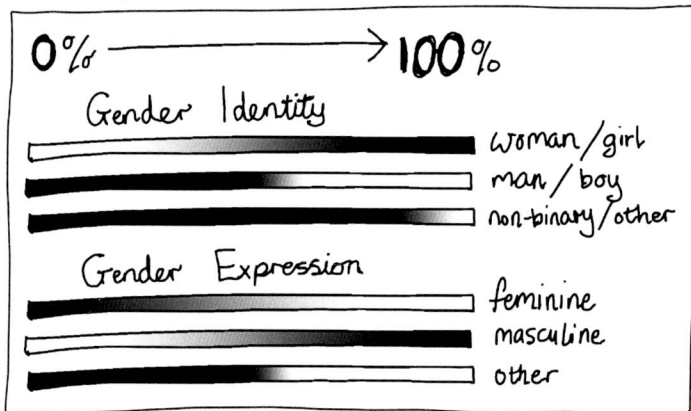

e.g.

0% ——————→ 100%

Gender Identity

woman/girl
man/boy
non-binary/other

Gender Expression

feminine
masculine
other

(sliders inspired by http://www.transstudent.org/gender)

our clothes are not
our gender

An illustration cannot accurately portray the complexities of gender. For example, it is hard to map **GENDER IDENTITY THAT CHANGES OVER TIME** or **PEOPLE EXPERIENCING TWO OR MORE VERY DIFFERENT GENDERS**. Illustrations such as these also fail to map cultural differences in gender identity. But hopefully these visualisations will help you to understand that

GENDER IS NOT AS SIMPLE AS WE ARE OFTEN LED TO BELIEVE.

Many people often think that non-binary people are gender neutral, but because gender is broad, there are many terms to describe someone's gender.

Some people identify with a very specific gender. Other people have genders that change with time or context. And other people experience two or more genders at once!

Other genders and identities are available.

HERE ARE A FEW TERMS THAT NON-BINARY PEOPLE MAY USE

DEMI BOY/GIRL Someone who identifies partially with the genders man/woman and partially with another identity.

GENDER FLUID Someone whose gender changes daily/monthly/yearly or depending on who they are with or where they are etc.

AGENDER Someone who does not experience gender or rejects the concept of gender.

(*Agender can be seen by some as a gender identity, even though it means a lack of gender.*)

Some agender people say they feel **NUMB** to gendered terms; they **DON'T CONNECT** with them and **DON'T RELATE** to them. Other agender people say they feel like an alien; very confused by the **STRICT BINARY GENDERS**.

BI/POLY GENDER Someone who experiences two or more genders, either at the same time or at different times.

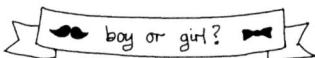

Some people **MIX AND MATCH** labels to be more specific or less specific, or they may use **DIFFERENT LABELS IN DIFFERENT PLACES.**

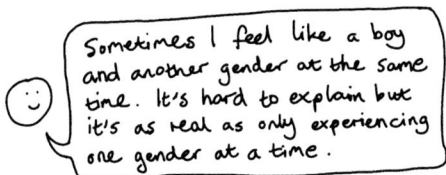

Sometimes I feel like a boy and another gender at the same time. It's hard to explain but it's as real as only experiencing one gender at a time.

There's no need to memorise all of these,

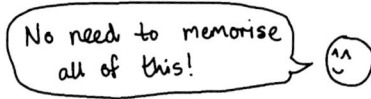

No need to memorise all of this!

but it helps to illustrate just how varied gender can be. Having words like this **HELPS NON-BINARY PEOPLE TO UNDERSTAND THEMSELVES BETTER**. It is probably more important for everyone else to know and respect someone's **PRONOUNS** than to know their precise **GENDER LABEL**. We explore this later.

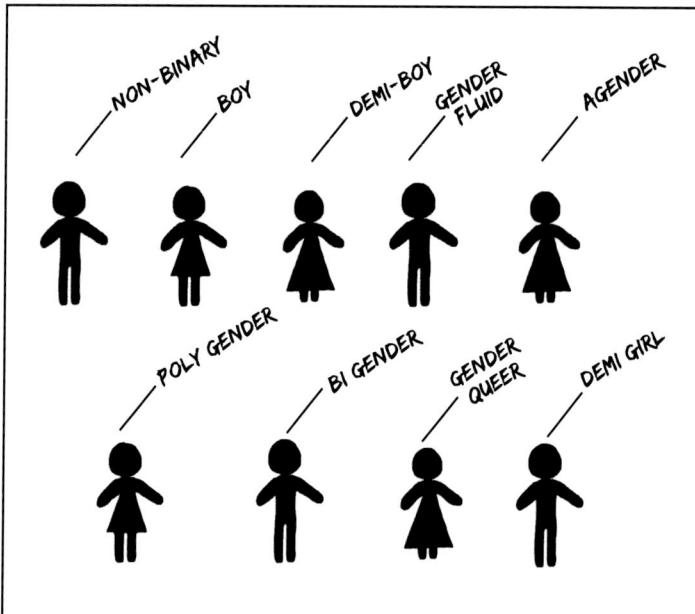

IS IT THE SAME AS BEING TRANS?

Trans is short for **TRANSGENDER**. It means to **NOT SOLELY IDENTIFY WITH THE GENDER YOU WERE ASSIGNED AT BIRTH.**

'TRANS' IS A LATIN PREFIX MEANING 'ACROSS'.

Cis is short for **CISGENDER.** This is the opposite of trans and means to identify with the gender you **WERE** assigned at birth.

'CIS' IS A LATIN PREFIX MEANING 'ON THE SAME SIDE'.

A common mistake people make is using the terms 'transgend*ered* and 'cisgend*ered*. These are incorrect as 'transgender' and 'cisgender' are **ADJECTIVES**, not verbs.

TRANS is often used as a term that covers trans men and women, as well as non-binary people. But **NOT ALL NON-BINARY PEOPLE CALL THEMSELVES TRANS**. Each person is different and has the right to use the labels they are most comfortable with.

Transness is often equated to some form of **MEDICAL TRANSITION**, such as hormones or surgery.

BUT THAT ISN'T WHAT MAKES SOMEONE TRANS. Neither is experiencing *dysphoria*, which is explained further in the following pages.

GENDER IDENTITY IS A PERSONAL FEELING AND SENSE OF SELF.

Gender identity is different to **GENDER EXPRESSION.** Gender expression is the way we present ourselves to the world.

All of us are taught to **RECOGNISE MEN AND WOMEN BY THE CLOTHES THEY WEAR.** For instance, dresses are associated with girls and women.

THIS IS A TRICK!

Clothes do not relate to someone's gender and people of any gender should be able to wear any clothes (and they do)! This is the same for other kinds of gender expression, such as shaving or growing body hair. **NONE OF THESE THINGS RELATE TO GENDER IDENTITY.**

This is important because:

SOME NON-BINARY PEOPLE MAY CHANGE THEIR PRESENTATION – change clothes, hair, or makeup etc.

Some non-binary people may change their presentation **AT PARTICULAR TIMES.**

SOME NON-BINARY PEOPLE MAY NOT CHANGE THEIR PRESENTATION. They may *'look like a girl/boy'* but this does not mean they ARE a girl or a boy!

Society has created unwritten rules about presentation and expectations of gender (cisnormativity). How useful are these?

It's important to remember that the things that teach us how to recognise men and women **CHANGE OVER TIME AND BETWEEN CULTURES.**

Did you know that **PINK** used to be a 'boys' colour and **BLUE** used to be a 'girls' colour?

Not to mention that women used to wear only dresses and skirts but now commonly wear trousers....

PRONOUNS

WHAT ARE PRONOUNS?

PRONOUNS ARE WORDS WE USE TO TALK ABOUT SOMEONE ELSE. They usually replace someone's name, but are often gendered. For example:

'Alex touches **his** hat as **he** looks at **himself** in the mirror.'

Using a name instead of pronouns can feel too repetitive and is not a common way to talk about someone.

'Alex touches **Alex's** hat as **Alex** looks at **Alex** in the mirror.'

(Although, some non-binary people do prefer if you use their name only, in place of pronouns.)

Non-binary people use **ALL KINDS OF PRONOUNS!** Some won't change their pronouns, some will change to 'he' or 'she'.

Many opt for a **NEUTRAL PRONOUN WE ARE ALREADY FAMILIAR WITH - 'THEY'.**

Some opt for **NEOPRONOUNS**. Some people's pronouns fluctuate, and that's ok too! Some people only use their name.

HOW TO USE DIFFERENT PRONOUNS

____ is so cool!	I like ____	That is ____ hat. That hat is ____.
She He They (are)	her him them	her/hers his their/theirs
Ze Ze E or Ey Per	hir zir em per	hir/hirs zir/zirs eir/eirs per/pers
Name	Name	Name's

(rows 2 and 3 are labelled **neopronouns** *on the left)*

TIPS

If you make a mistake with someone's pronouns, **CORRECT YOURSELF AND MOVE ON!**

When meeting new people, ask what pronoun they use! If you don't feel comfortable doing this then you can use their name or "they" pronouns until you hear someone who knows them well use their pronouns.

DYSPHORIA

GENDER DYSPHORIA is discomfort brought on by a mismatch either between your **GENDER IDENTITY** and society's view of your gender, or between your **BODY MAP** and your body. Body map is the sense in your brain of what your body is like.

Dysphoria can be both **MENTALLY AND PHYSICALLY PAINFUL**, as well as incredibly distressing.

There are different kinds of dysphoria relating to gender. The one that most people are familiar with is **BODY OR PHYSICAL DYSPHORIA**. This is when a person feels a disconnect, disgust or distress over parts of their body. These are often parts that they feel **ASSOCIATE THEM WITH AN INCORRECT GENDER.**

There is also **SOCIAL DYSPHORIA**. This occurs when someone is misgendered or seen as the wrong gender by other people. This can be just as painful as physical dysphoria.

Not every trans or non-binary person experiences dysphoria, but **INVALIDATION OF ONES GENDER(S) OVER A PERIOD OF TIME CAN STILL HAVE NEGATIVE EFFECTS.**

EUPHORIA

GENDER EUPHORIA is the opposite of dysphoria.

IT'S THE AMAZING FEELING YOU MIGHT EXPERIENCE WHEN SOMEONE GENDERS YOU CORRECTLY, or when you're wearing something that makes you feel valid in your own gender.

Not every trans or non-binary person experiences euphoria.

Sometimes, when someone is questioning their gender, **EXPERIENCING GENDER EUPHORIA IS THE FIRST TIME THAT THEY FEEL VALID**.

Some kind of transition often helps to alleviate dysphoria or increase euphoria. **SOMETIMES THIS IS JUST ASKING FOR THE RIGHT PRONOUNS** with no change to presentation. Sometimes it is a change in **CLOTHES AND HAIRCUT**. Sometimes it involves taking medical steps. Some people choose to change nothing; simply understanding their gender better is helpful enough.

All of these approaches are valid and there is no right or wrong way to live your life once you have explored your gender. **EVERYONE'S APPROACH IS UNIQUE.**

GLOSSARY

AGENDER: Someone who does not have a gender, does not experience gender, or rejects the concept of gender

BI/POLY GENDER: Someone who experiences two or more genders, either at the same time or at different times.

CISGENDER: Someone who wholly identifies with the gender they were assigned at birth – often shortened to cis.

DEMI BOY/GIRL: Someone who identifies partially with the genders man/woman and partially with another identity.

GENDER DYSPHORIA: Intense feelings of discomfort/disgust, pain, or hopelessness in relation to your body, your gender identity or your expression.

GENDER EUPHORIA: Intense feelings of comfort and happiness in relation to your gender identity or expression.

GENDER FLUID: Someone whose gender changes daily/monthly/yearly or depending on who they are with or where they are etc.

GENDER IDENTITY: The gender that makes you who you are.

GENDERQUEER: Someone who does not wholly identify with the genders of man or woman. An older term that is often used in the same way as "non-binary". However, it is a distinct identity that has a more political connotation.

MAVERIQUE: Someone who experiences a feeling of gender that is independent of man or woman

NEUTROIS: A neutral gender, often described as being between man and woman, but also sometimes meaning genderless.

NON-BINARY: Someone who does not wholly identify with the genders of man or woman.

SEX TRAITS: The various characteristics that are typically associated with your sex e.g. external sex characteristics (genitals), secondary sex characteristics, internal sex organs, chromosomes, hormones

TRANSGENDER: Someone who does not wholly identify with the gender they were assigned at birth – often shortened to trans. However this term is more often used to describe binary trans people who are transitioning between the binary genders of man and woman.

HOWEVER, DON'T FORGET THAT NON-BINARY PEOPLE CAN BE TRANS TOO!

HOW SHOULD I SUPPORT NON-BINARY PEOPLE?

DO

- Use their name and pronouns
- Remember they are still the same person.
- Check their feelings on gendered words such as – daughter, brother, mrs, sir.
- Check who they are 'out' to and how to refer to them with people who may not know.
- With people who do know, correct their mistakes.
- Understand identity can shift – their pronouns or labels might change.
- Do your own research, find out more, and learn.
- Understand that you will never be able to empathise from their perspective.

DO NOT

- Ask about their genitals (more common than you'd think!)
- Ask about their sex life.
- Confuse gender with sexuality – trans and gay are not synonymous. (Also transitioning doesn't automatically change someone's sexuality.)
- Ask if they're sure – they will have thought about this a lot before speaking to you.
- Tell them that non-binary doesn't exist – they are literally existing in front of you!
- Call it a phase.
- Think they are just trying to be special.
- Get upset or defensive if you are corrected or a non-binary person asks you to be more inclusive.
- Use phrases that exclude non-binary people e.g. Ladies and Gentlemen, 'he or she' in text.

NON-BINARY NOTES

Name(s): _____

_____

Pronouns: _____

I Identify as:

_____

Terms not to use for me:

_____

_____

Who knows about this:

_____

Should you use my new
info with new people?

_____

_____

Notes:

Terms to use instea[d]

_____

_____

_____

Who should NOT kno[w]

_____

Are there any
exceptions?

_____

_____

Anything else?

If you are non-binary: fill this in to **INFORM** your friends and family.
If you are not non-binary: ask a **NON-BINARY FRIEND** if they would mind
it in to better inform you. Why not photocopy? ☺